ROCK & ROLL
HALL OF FAMERS

Stevie Wonder

MARK BEYER

the rosen publishing group's
rosen
central

3 9063 10007 9535

FEB 1 1 2005

To Stevie Wonder, who has been an inspiration to millions.

Published in 2002 by The Rosen Publishing Group, Inc.
29 East 21st Street, New York, NY 10010

Library of Congress Cataloging-in-Publication Data

Beyer, Mark (Mark T.)
Stevie Wonder/by Mark Beyer.1st ed.
p. cm. — (Rock & roll hall of famers)
Includes discography, directory of Web sites, bibliographical references, and index.
ISBN 0-8239-3525-6 (library binding)
1. Wonder, Stevie—Juvenile literature. 2. Rock musicians—United States–Biography—Juvenile literature. [1.Wonder, Stevie. 2. Musicians. 3. Composers. 4. Afro-Americans—Biography. 5. Blind. 6. Physically handicapped.]
I. Title. II. Series.
ML3930.W65 B49 2002
782.421644'092—dc21

2001003609

Manufactured in the United States of America

CONTENTS

Stevie Wonder thrills audiences during South African president Nelson Mandela's seventieth birthday.

Introduction

Stevie Wonder has been blind his entire life. He lives in a world of visual darkness. His music, however, has colored the world with brightness, joy, and hope. From his humble beginnings in Saginaw, Michigan, Stevie quickly rose to musical stardom. At thirteen years old, he was the youngest star at Motown Records. By the age of twenty-one, Stevie Wonder was known throughout the world as a musical genius. His genius goes beyond music, however. Stevie is also an outspoken civil rights activist, a political voice, and a person who brings different races in America together. Stevie's musical harmony also helped to bring some harmony to the American cultural map. Today, Stevie Wonder continues to write, produce records, and play to audiences around the world. His life has been an inspiration to musicians around the globe.

The story of Stevie Wonder is not all happiness, fame, and fortune, however. He has suffered from his blindness in ways no sighted person can imagine. He also dealt with racial prejudice, business conflicts, and broken relationships. Stevie's sense of humor and his music have kept him strong through it all. Sound has been his friend and ally since before he realized he was very different from most everyone else. In Stevie's words, though, his blindness has been a "blessing and a virtue."

By the age of thirteen, Stevie Wonder was already a big star.

And for the audience that has cherished his voice, lyrics, and music for nearly forty years, Stevie Wonder has an ability to see the world like few others of his generation.

The World in Darkness

Stevie Wonder remembers when he first became aware that he was blind. Stevie said, "I'd be wallowing around in the grass back of the house, and I'd get myself and my clothes soiled. My mother would get on me about that. She explained that I couldn't move about so much, that I'd have to try and stay in one place."

This was when Stevie was about five years old. Keeping a five-year-old in one place might be the hardest thing any parent can try to do. Lulu Hardaway, Stevie's mother, wasn't very successful. When Stevie did stay in one place, he used to jump up and down. This was his way of knowing that the world was around him. He wanted to be part of the world. He needed sound to understand how the world worked. Stevie used his hearing to identify with that world.

"There's one thing you gotta remember about sound," Stevie said. "Sound happens all the time, all the time. If you put your hands right up to your ears, if you close your eyes and move your hands back and forth, you can hear the sound getting closer and farther away. Sound bounces off everything, there's always something happening." Although he was blind, Stevie Wonder knew early in his life that sound was going to help him to learn, live, and succeed.

Miracle Baby

Stevie Wonder was born on May 13, 1950, in Saginaw, Michigan. His birth name was Steveland Morris, and he was the third son of Lulu Mae Hardaway. Stevie's two older half brothers, Calvin and Milton, were sons of Lulu's first husband. Any confusion between fathers has been explained by Stevie like this: "I have a lovely mother and she was fortunate enough to be married to more than one man."

Lulu was the head of the household in Saginaw. Her first husband left the family shortly after Milton was born. Stevie's own father left his mother and the three boys shortly after Stevie was born. Lulu's three sons had no father for the three years that they lived in Saginaw. Lulu cleaned houses to earn money for the family.

Stevie was born one month before he was due. His premature birth was hard on his infant body. Back then, the regular course of action was to put a premature baby in an incubator. An incubator gives a baby oxygen until it can breathe on its own. When Stevie was taken out of the incubator, he was blind. "I have a dislocated nerve in one eye," Stevie explained. "A cataract [milky film] is on the other. It may have happened from being in the incubator too long and receiving too much oxygen." Doctors did not know the effects of pure oxygen on infants at the time. "A girl who was born that same day I was," Stevie said, "was also put into the incubator, and she died. I personally think I'm lucky to be alive."

His Own Way of Seeing

The medical name for Stevie's blindness is retrolental fibroplasia. It is caused by giving too much oxygen to infants who must live in an incubator after birth. This type of blindness cannot be corrected through surgery. Stevie Wonder would never be able to see his hands, green leaves on a tree, the blue sky, or the white and black keys on a piano.

"In my mind I can see all these things in my own way," Stevie said. Blind people do have their own way of seeing, of course. They use touch and sound. They also use a heightened sense of inner feeling. In fact, all blind people use their other senses to compensate for their handicap. Sighted people can see expressions on people's faces, but blind people can just as easily understand people's feelings through the sound of their voice. Sound becomes the

Myths About Blindness

Many cultures have viewed blindness as a sort of gift. Those who could not see with their eyes were thought to have other special abilities. One was an ability to see into the future. Another was the ability to play music well. This is completely false, of course. There are many blind people that can't sing a tune any better than a sighted person who lacks that same ability.

most important sense to someone who is blind. It is his or her connection to the outside world. Steveland Morris understood this before he completely understood that he was blind.

Detroit and Change

In 1953, Lulu moved with her three boys to Detroit, Michigan. She got back together with

Paul Hardaway (Milton and Calvin's father). The reunited family lived in Detroit's east side black ghetto. Paul began work in a bagel factory. Lulu cleaned the houses of wealthy people. The family made a living in Detroit, and life became better for them. They were still poor, but the family

Stevie Wonder's hometown of Detroit, Michigan, circa 1950

was stable and happy. Eventually, Lulu and Paul would have three more children. Two boys followed Stevie, and the siblings' only sister came later.

Lulu feared for Stevie's safety when they first moved to Detroit. Getting used to change is difficult for anyone who is blind. For a three-year-old boy, this changed his entire world. Detroit was larger, more crowded, and busier with street traffic. Stevie had to get used to a new house and neighborhood. He had to learn where furniture was placed and where the different rooms were in the house. Lulu's fear of Stevie getting hurt forced her to keep him inside the house most of the time. Stevie had only his brothers to play with. Stevie's only world was his family and the sounds, smells, and objects inside their home.

Stevie used what was around him to learn all that he could. Sound was most important, followed by touch and smell. Stevie used his memory to learn where furniture was. He also used his memory of sound to learn more about the world around him. Stevie recalled, "I remember people dropping money on the table and saying, 'What's that, Steve?' … I could almost always get it right, except a penny and a nickel confused me."

Lulu watched Stevie's progress closely. Even so, Stevie continued walking into furniture and getting into trouble when he soiled his clothes while playing in the yard. Stevie began walking with his arms straight out to guard against walking into things. His mother told him to stop doing that. She thought he looked foolish. She also knew inside that people would laugh at Stevie if they saw him walking this way. Lulu didn't want Stevie to feel humiliated for being blind. She told him that he must not move around too much. This is when Stevie began to jump up and down a lot. He listened to his feet hit the floor. He listened to the echo his stamping feet made against the walls. Stevie began to learn about echoes and distance.

To encourage Stevie not to move around so much, Lulu bought him a cardboard drum to play with. Stevie had already been hitting things to hear what sound they made. Now he had a drum to bang on. Stevie hit the drum for hours. "I'd beat 'em to death," Stevie remembered.

Using Sound to See the World

When Stevie was seven years old, a doctor explained his blindness to him. Up until that time, Stevie thought that other people banged into furniture less than he did because they were older. They knew where tables and furniture

15

were placed, and he needed to learn this, too. Stevie was wrong, of course. He soon realized that he would always need to be careful about how and where he walked.

Stevie understood sound much better by this time. He used sound to help him do things. He taught himself how sound could tell him where objects were and how far away he was from these objects. This method is called sonar. Stevie would call out and listen for an echo. The echo from his voice bounced off a nearby object. Stevie knew how far away an object was by

Fun Fact!

When Stevie was two years old, his favorite instrument was the spoons. He used to hold the spoons and hit them against his leg. He began to use the spoons as drumsticks, and went around the house hitting everything.

the sound of the echo. Everyone has this ability, but sighted people don't need to use it. Blind people, however, train themselves to use their sonar. All blind children develop this sense between the ages of one and three.

Using sound and touch, Stevie now easily moved around the house. He began to play outside with his brothers. Calvin and Milton knew that Stevie could not see with his eyes like they could. Stevie, however, used his hands and the sounds coming to him from all around to move about freely. Stevie began to climb trees and ride a bicycle (with someone holding the handlebars to steer). Like any child, Stevie took chances. His blindness did little to hold him back from playing with his brothers and friends. Their favorite game was to jump from one woodshed roof to another. Calvin and Milton judged the distance by sight, of course. Stevie crouched at the edge of one roof and called out. His voice sounded different depending on how far away the next roof was.

"I know it used to worry my mother," Stevie remembered of his childhood games, "and I know she prayed for me to have sight someday, and so finally I just told her that I was happy being blind, and I thought it was a gift from God, and I think she felt better after that."

Schooltime

Stevie attended special classes for the blind when he entered school. The Detroit public school system was poor, but it had good teachers that helped handicapped children especially well. A special bus picked up Stevie each morning and brought him home in the afternoon. Stevie was learning how to adjust to life outside his home. He needed this specialized training if he was going to succeed in life. Even though he'd come to rely on sound, touch, and smell, he needed to be taught how better to use each of these senses.

Speech lessons helped improve his speaking ability. Speaking is much more difficult for blind people than for sighted people. Sighted babies can watch how a mouth forms to make an "o" sound. They can see someone's tongue press against the front teeth to form the "th" sound. Without special instruction, blind children often are much older when they learn how to speak well.

Another important lesson Stevie learned was to use facial expressions. Humans use facial expressions all the time. Facial expressions describe moods and emotions. They also show physical feeling as

Stevie learned to use facial expressions to help him communicate.

well. Facial expressions are sighted people's silent communication. Blind babies naturally show facial expressions. They laugh and cry. They also show emotions physically. In time, however, these expressions stop because they cannot see that other people use these same expressions to communicate. Expressions are not a part of a blind baby's learning experience, and so they become "silent faces." Stevie was taught

1950
Steveland Morris is born on May 13.

1953
Stevie moves with his mother, Lulu, and two half brothers, Calvin and Milton, to Detroit, Michigan.

1955
Lulu gives Stevie his first instrument, a cardboard drum.

1959
Stevie learns to play the harmonica, drums, and piano; he also joins the church choir.

1962
Ronnie White helps Stevie get an audition with Hitsville USA. Stevie records his first song, "Mother, Thank You."

1963
Stevie records a live version of "Fingertips" and the single reaches number one. Stevie begins touring and also enters the Michigan School for the Blind.

1965
Stevie begins recording his own songs and the songs of other artists.

1970
Stevie marries Syreeta Wright. They stay married for a year and a half.

1971
Stevie turns twenty-one and leaves Motown Records to start his own record company.

1984
Stevie becomes active in American politics by backing Jesse Jackson for president.

1996
Stevie receives the Lifetime Achievement Award at the Grammy Awards.

1985
The song "I Just Called to Say I Love You" wins Stevie an Oscar.

1973
A car crash leaves Stevie with a severe head injury and he almost loses his life.

2001
Stevie performs at a free concert in Detroit to celebrate the city's 300th anniversary.

1974
Stevie marries Yolanda Simmons; Stevie wins his first Grammy Award (five in total that year).

1989
Stevie Wonder is inducted into the Rock and Roll Hall of Fame.

to show emotion in his face. He smiled when he felt happy and frowned when he was confused. Stevie learned how to act "normally."

Stevie's sense of touch was already well developed. He already knew the difference between grass and dirt, concrete and rock, and wood and metal. Stevie needed to increase his sensitivity to touch. He would use that touch to learn to read braille. Frenchman Louis Braille invented this reading system, which uses a system of dots raised on a surface. The number of dots and their position correspond to a letter or sound. Stevie also learned how to use a braille typewriter, so that he could write letters. Reading opened a whole other world to Stevie. He loved to read, and he also listened to books that were recorded on records.

Listening and making sound was everything to Stevie's dark world. Without sound, there was no world. If you cut off a blind person's ability to hear, you cut them off from life. Stevie hated silence, and so he made noise. He soon began to turn that noise into music.

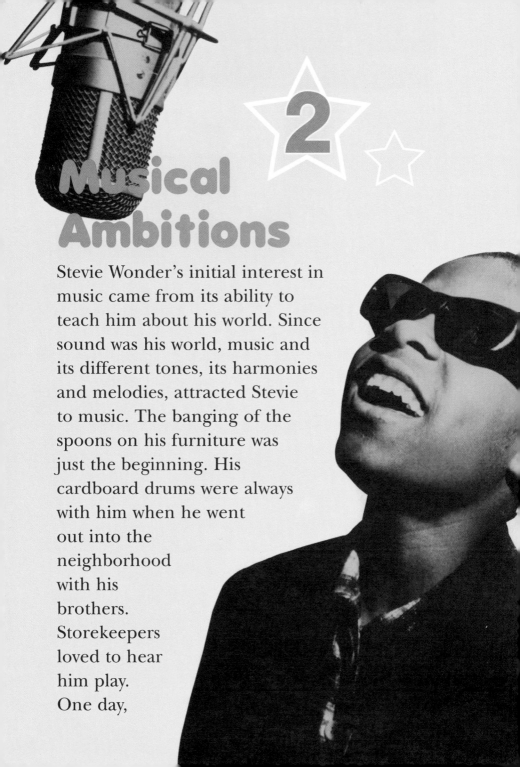

Musical Ambitions

2

Stevie Wonder's initial interest in music came from its ability to teach him about his world. Since sound was his world, music and its different tones, its harmonies and melodies, attracted Stevie to music. The banging of the spoons on his furniture was just the beginning. His cardboard drums were always with him when he went out into the neighborhood with his brothers. Storekeepers loved to hear him play. One day, the neighborhood barber gave Stevie a small, four-note harmonica to put on his key chain. Stevie now had a new instrument to play. He played his mini harmonica like no one had ever heard before. Stevie was able to get a huge range of sound from the little instrument. Stevie's hunger for music was huge.

Radio Days

Being blind, Stevie had to entertain himself a lot. He had few friends at school. Even among the blind kids, separate groups developed. Some of them could see a little bit and this made them think they were better than the totally blind kids. The sighted kids at the school all whispered when the blind kids passed. Stevie heard all of their whispers. Even as an adult, Stevie couldn't understand how sighted people could be in a room with him and talk about him and his being blind. Didn't they realize that he wasn't deaf?

Stevie liked to listen to the radio when he was at home. He listened to a Detroit rhythm and blues (R & B) station that played B. B. King. He listened

The Drifters, pictured here, were one of Stevie Wonder's favorite vocal groups.

to many other black guitarists and singers. He knew their sounds and voices, and could pick out the different instruments that were being played. When he entered school, Stevie was given a transistor radio all his own. He was overjoyed! He listened to the radio while riding the bus to school and after school at home. Stevie even put the radio beneath his pillow while he slept at night.

"I liked the Five Royales, Johnny Ace, Clyde McPhatter, Jackie Wilson, Jimmy Reed, the Drifters," Stevie recalled. "Oh, Jimmy Reed. Oh, I used to love that boy, I swear. Oh the music! Jumping around and dancing. And the Coasters, the Dixie Hummingbirds, the Staple Singers—oooh!"

Early Instruments

When Stevie was six years old, he received a gift that would change his life. That year, the Detroit Lions Club, a community organization, presented Stevie with a real drum kit as a Christmas gift. He practiced the drums every day. He would play his harmonica and then play the drums. He began to play parts of songs that he remembered from listening to the radio. Stevie played the beats of the songs on the drums and the melodies on the harmonica. He soon mastered both instruments. This was quite an accomplishment for a six-year-old boy. In fact, for a six-year-old blind boy, Stevie was somewhat of a sensation

From drums, to harmonica, to piano, Stevie mastered many instruments while still a child.

around the front porches of the neighborhood. People asked him to play his harmonica as they sang lyrics. Stevie played the drums while others played guitar or a real, full-size harmonica. Music was becoming everything to Stevie, outside of his family and learning in school.

All the neighbors admired Stevie's musical talents. One woman from the neighborhood owned a piano. When she moved away, she decided to give the piano to Stevie. "I kept asking," Stevie remembered, "'When they gonna bring the piano over, Mamma?' I never realized how important that was going to be to me."

Stevie ran his hands all over the piano on the day it arrived. He felt the top, sides, and legs. He studied the wood with his hands, measuring the instrument in his mind. He touched the foot petals and felt they were metal. He ran his hands over the keys and found that some were raised. He asked his mother to let him feel the strings. Stevie ran his hands up and down the metal strings and over the hammers. Everything felt good to him.

Wonderful Music

Along with the drums, harmonica, and piano, Stevie began to sing. He loved voices, and from a young age was able to tell who was in the room from the sound of his or her voice. He had also learned the different calls of birds and was able to tell who was singing on the radio. Stevie loved all voices and music, and he began training his voice to sing along to radio tunes.

Lulu was part of the church choir, but never thought of herself as a musician. None of her family had ever been musically inclined, except for Stevie. He began to sing in the choir. Everyone discovered that he had a beautiful voice. They weren't surprised, though. His musical talents were already widely known. Stevie sang solo parts in the choir. He was also asked to sing at special events.

Along with choir singing, Stevie began to sing on neighborhood porches. People would give him quarters to sing or play his harmonica. When people began giving him dollar bills, he said he'd rather have the quarters, because they made noise in his pocket!

Did You Know?

While listening to the radio, Stevie learned to separate the sounds of each instrument he heard. Later, he learned to play all the instruments that he had heard in the songs he listened to.

At night Stevie listened to the WCHB radio program *Sundown*. He learned the tunes in his head every night. He played the notes on the piano, drums, and harmonica every day. "I played Jimmy Reed's blues," Stevie recalled. "Bobby Blue Bland's. I used to sit by the radio and listen till sunup. Took a little of everybody's style and made it my own."

A Detroit Record

When Stevie was twelve years old, he had many friends who played music and sang. One of his musician friends was named John Glover. They used to play harmonica and sing together. John Glover had a cousin, Ronnie White, who lived in another part of Detroit. Ronnie White sang with a group called the Miracles. John Glover told his cousin Ronnie about a kid he knew named Steveland Morris. Ronnie didn't believe that a twelve-year-old boy could sing and play instruments as well as John claimed. John asked Ronnie to come around the neighborhood some time to see (and hear!) Steveland for himself. One day Ronnie did just that. Of course, Stevie was jamming on the front porch, as usual. Ronnie was blown away by the kid's voice and music style. Steveland Morris was about to get a great chance to become a recording artist.

The Miracles had a record contract with Hitsville USA. Ronnie White knew the president of Hitsville USA, Berry Gordy Jr. White called Gordy and told him about this kid he'd heard all about and finally had listened to himself. He suggested to Gordy that he give Steveland Morris an audition.

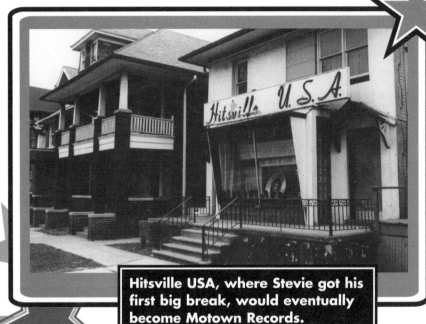

Hitsville USA, where Stevie got his first big break, would eventually become Motown Records.

Stevie's parents took him down to the Hitsville USA studios for his audition. Ronnie White met them and gave Stevie a tour of the studio. He let Stevie play different instruments. Stevie asked the name of each instrument he picked up and played. Stevie thought he'd gone to heaven. This was where he wanted to be!

Berry Gordy was excited to meet Steveland Morris. He sat in the studio and listened to Stevie play the bongos and sing. Gordy remembered that day clearly: "He was playing the bongos and singing, doing very well. I didn't even know at the time that he could play harmonica as well as he could. I knew that he was very talented. I heard him sing and I felt that there was a uniqueness in his voice."

After Stevie sang for Gordy, the Hitsville USA president wanted to hire this boy genius immediately. Stevie's parents were thrilled. There wasn't a lot of talk about money. They saw this as a great opportunity for Stevie. He might never get an opportunity like this again. The fact that a successful record company wanted to give this twelve-year-old blind boy a chance to write, play, and record music was the best part of the deal. Because Stevie was a minor (under eighteen years old), his mother signed the contract. The Hitsville USA recording studio would be the place where Stevie spent most of his time over the next ten years.

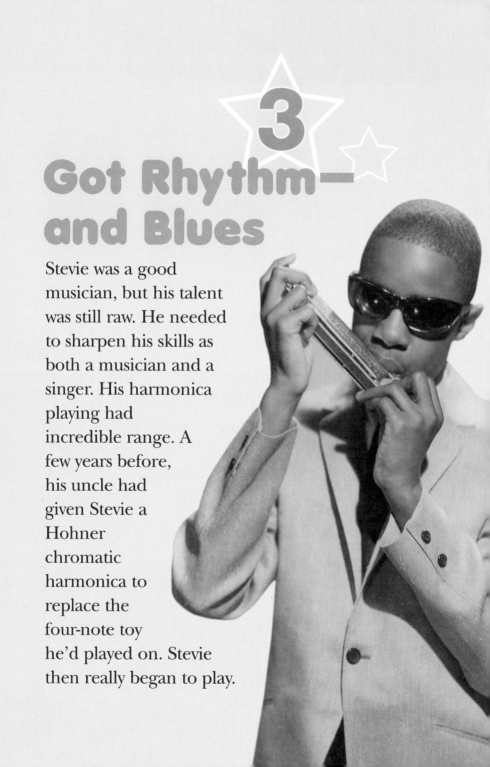

Got Rhythm— and Blues

3

Stevie was a good
musician, but his talent
was still raw. He needed
to sharpen his skills as
both a musician and a
singer. His harmonica
playing had
incredible range. A
few years before,
his uncle had
given Stevie a
Hohner
chromatic
harmonica to
replace the
four-note toy
he'd played on. Stevie
then really began to play.

He used his hearing to pull every note he could from that harmonica. Now, it seemed his practice was paying off. What you and I might call practice was not how Stevie saw his music playing. "I never considered it practice because I loved it too much," he remembered. "It was like searching in a new place you've never been before. I kept finding new things, new chords, new tunes."

Stevie had to balance his school with his budding music career. He'd go to school until three o'clock and then be driven to the Hitsville USA studios to play and record. Stevie was a rhythm and blues musician. That's the kind of music he'd listened to for seven years already. Rhythm and blues is what he mimicked from the radio. He'd developed his own style from learning to play tunes he'd heard on the air. Hitsville USA didn't want Stevie to change his playing. They did, however, want him to learn their musical style.

Studio Sound

In the 1950s and 1960s, each record company hired musicians that played a similar kind of

Berry Gordy Jr., the founder of Motown Records

music. Hitsville USA had recording contracts with groups that played a smooth, upbeat rhythm and blues. Most of the songs produced by Hitsville USA were about love and had a good beat. Kids listening to the radio and buying albums and singles could dance to this kind of music. Berry Gordy wanted Steveland Morris to write and record these kinds of songs.

When Stevie began to work on his music at Hitsville USA, he played all different kinds of instruments. The instruments he hadn't learned in his neighborhood were quickly mastered in the studio. He learned the saxophone and trumpet. He played around with flutes and clarinets. He also learned to play the organ. All these instruments helped Stevie create his own sound and musical style.

Stevie had borrowed a lot from other musicians' music styles. But Stevie was his own musician. Even at the young age of twelve, he wasn't simply going to roll over and do what the record producers wanted. Instead, he developed his own style while he listened to what the producers had to say. They gave him plenty of advice on how to write and what to write about. They also had many suggestions about Stevie's musical arrangements. Stevie would listen and smile, and he'd thank the producers for their suggestions. He learned their style, but also made that style into his own. Stevie never wanted to imitate what the other artists were recording. In fact, the first two songs he wrote while working at Hitsville USA were concertos. Stevie liked concertos because the music was played around a soloist. Of course, Stevie always saw himself as the soloist, accompanied by an orchestra behind him.

Within a year, Stevie had perfected his own sound. It was a Hitsville USA sound, but he had to begin somewhere. "When we first started out we did a lot of standard tunes," Stevie remembered. "[They] were never released because [Hitsville USA] wanted a single." Almost all of those early recordings are lost to us today. They caught Stevie when he was raw and trying all different kinds of musical arrangements. "The first thing I ever recorded was [a song] called 'Mother, Thank You,'" Stevie recalled, "which originally was called 'You Made a Vow.' They felt that 'You Made a Vow' was too much a love song for me and they decided to change it."

"Mother, Thank You" was released but sold very few copies. Stevie didn't mind. He was happy that something of his was recorded. His next recording was "I Call It Pretty Music" in August 1962. Again, the single sold few copies, but it showed Stevie's talent and potential. Stevie's voice and music were out there. His time was going to come.

Wonder Boy

In late 1963, Stevie recorded a live version of the song "Fingertips." Stevie did not write "Fingertips,"

STEVIE WONDER

FROM HIS ALBUM STEVIE AT THE BEACH — TAMLA 255

TAMLA 54096

The cover for the single "Hey Harmonica Man," from an early recording called _Stevie at the Beach_

but he showed the record producers what he could do with his musical talents. Stevie had been playing concerts for Hitsville USA promoters for months. He was on the bill with other Hitsville artists. The Hitsville producers were still trying to figure out how to market this preteen talent.

Stevie played much better in front of an audience. His studio recordings were good, but in front of a crowd Stevie really shined. Stevie was especially animated while performing "Fingertips." This song had Stevie playing harmonica and singing mostly "yeah, yeah, yeah" over and over. But the way Stevie sang the song drove audiences crazy. Gordy decided to record Stevie singing "Fingertips" and other songs while at Chicago's Regal Theatre. Some of the songs were OK, but "Fingertips" and "La La La La La" were out of this world! Stevie got the crowd clapping and singing along to "Fingertips." Stevie improvised his harmonica solo and drew the song out long and smooth. The live version of "Fingertips" was far better than the studio version.

Hitsville USA thought the beat was great and the screaming just enough to excite a teenage crowd. The producers decided to promote the song heavily. To help the song catch on with the public, they wanted Steveland Morris to change

Young Stevie Wonder was known for putting on a great live show.

his name. Hitsville USA wanted a hit name to go with what they hoped would be a hit song.

Stevie had been around the studio for more than a year already. His talent was well known among the producers and recording technicians. Stevie's conductor, Clarence Paul, called him Little Stevie. He was also known as "the little boy wonder." When someone suggested the name Little Stevie Wonder, Berry Gordy liked the sound. "They didn't like 'Steve Morris,'" Stevie remembered. "So they changed it." Stevie liked his own name, but he

Fun Fact!

At thirteen, Stevie often lost himself in his music while performing for audiences. Sometimes his manager had to go on stage and carry Stevie off.

was a recording artist and did what the record company wanted.

A Chart Topper

"Fingertips" was released to the public as a single in the summer of 1963. Stevie had just turned thirteen years old. The Hitsville USA producers watched as the single sold thousands of copies. "Fingertips" rose up the charts and hit number one. It stayed at number one for fifteen weeks. It eventually sold more than one million copies. No one expected such a huge response to the single. Little Stevie Wonder was an instant celebrity.

"Fingertips" was the highest selling record of Berry Gordy's producing career. The single made Hitsville USA a sudden success. Within a year, Gordy changed the record studio's name from Hitsville USA to Motown. Motown is a combined name of Motor Town. Motor Town was Detroit's nickname because the auto industry made most of America's cars there. Motown records would soon sign some of the greatest recording artists known throughout the world.

Meanwhile, Motown needed to send Stevie Wonder out on tour. They also wanted him to record more songs. An album needed to be released soon to back up the single "Fingertips." The concert tour would promote the album. This was all such a rush for everyone at Motown, including Stevie Wonder. Stevie tried to take all of this excitement in stride. He was happy that a single of his had finally done well. More important, he was singing and writing songs, and was surrounded by people who understood him. They wanted to help him become a successful musician.

4

Coming of Age at Motown

Stevie Wonder may have been a star at thirteen, but he was still a boy. The law said that he had to stay in school. Stevie wanted to stay in school and learn, of course, but he also wanted to record songs and perform at concerts. The schedule between school and his career was difficult. At one point, the state of Michigan said he must be in school every weekday. But that would have harmed Stevie's career.

Stevie needed to be at the Motown recording studios most days of the week. He also needed to be traveling around the country and singing. Albums sold well when musicians performed in concert. If his albums didn't sell, then Stevie's music career would fail quickly. Something had to be worked out with his schooling schedule that allowed him to continue recording and touring.

Managing Music and School

"When the people at the Board of Education said that I couldn't perform," Stevie recalled, "[and] the Detroit schools couldn't accommodate my wanting to go on the road . . . I cried and cried and prayed for a long time."

Stevie's parents were more concerned than Motown executives about Stevie's education. A music career was nice, they thought, but Stevie still had a lot of schooling to complete. In fact, Stevie had much more to learn than other children. His blindness was not going to go away. Stevie needed to learn how to cope in the world.

He could learn this best from teachers of the blind.

Finally, a solution to the problem was found. Stevie left the Detroit public school system and enrolled in the Michigan School for the Blind. Motown paid for a tutor from the school to be with Stevie on all the tours. Stevie performed mostly one-night

Stevie Wonder during a quiet moment on tour

stands with other Motown musicians. They traveled to different states for weeks at a time. Ted Hall was Stevie's tutor on these trips. Hall and Stevie became friends and companions quickly. Hall spent the next six years traveling with—and tutoring—Stevie.

"Motown recruited me," Hall recalled. "They did a nationwide search looking for a suitable tutor for Stevie. I was totally in charge of

47

Stevie's day-to-day activities. The company, working through a booking agent, would consult with me and set up a tour. Then it was my job to provide Stevie's educational needs as coordinated through the School for the Blind."

If you think that Stevie had it easy with Hall, think again. Stevie wasn't in a real classroom, yet he had plenty of work to do. Hall came to work with Stevie in September of 1963. He quickly developed a plan for Stevie's schoolwork that organized Stevie's life by every hour in the day.

"We would travel throughout the country or around the world with a lot of activities," Hall explained. "I was paid by Motown, and the management part of Stevie's program was directed by Motown. All I had to go on was my own childhood, and so I established an allowance with Stevie and I worked it out with his parents so he didn't develop champagne tastes at too early an age. It seemed to work very well. He seems to appreciate it now, but he didn't appreciate it at all at the time."

The money that Stevie made from his record sales went into a bank trust account. Except for expenses, Stevie could not touch what he earned (and neither could anyone else!) until he reached the age of twenty-one. His allowance began at $2.50 per week. On tour, Stevie did not need much. He wanted to buy musical instruments, but Motown said no. He often ran out of his allowance. What Stevie bought most with his small allowance were gifts for his mother. He missed her a lot, and they spoke on the phone nearly every night. As far away as Stevie sometimes traveled from home, he was always close to his mother in mind and heart.

Stevie worked tirelessly at his schoolwork and his musical ambitions. "He held out extremely well," Hall remembered, "and I always recognized that Stevie was holding down two full-time jobs, one as a student and the other as an entertainer. I don't think he realized it. We wouldn't start school until about ten o'clock in the morning, but I would get up at 6 AM usually to prepare for school [and] try to get a head start on the kid. Then we would have school for three and a half to four hours and then it would be the entertainment business until maybe twelve or one o'clock in the evening."

Time didn't mean much to Stevie. Time doesn't mean much to any blind person. Because the blind cannot see either the light or dark of each day, they don't live by the same concept of time and the clock as do sighted people. In fact, Stevie was famous around Motown for his tardiness. Some people wondered if Stevie was somehow rebelling in a way for all the work he was doing for Motown. He was always being told what to do; he also could do little on his own because he was blind. On the road, Stevie was constantly in unfamiliar surroundings. He couldn't just get up and go outside to walk around the block. Stevie always needed some kind of companion. Being late was one way Stevie showed his independence from his structured life.

Short Homecomings

When Stevie did come home to attend the School for the Blind, he proved that he was always prepared. Stevie's intelligence allowed him to

Did You Know?

One activity that Stevie Wonder enjoys is roller-skating. He has never let his blindness keep him from having fun.

quickly pick up his classes where he had left off. His on-the-road studies had prepared him well for every in-class subject. "When I did go back to school," Stevie remembered, "they had everything, like swimming, boating, skating. I was on the wrestling team for a while, on the track team for a while, we got into various outside activities. I was more interested in music. But it was a challenge."

One challenge at which Stevie succeeded was having a social life at the school. He made many friends, some of whom are still good friends today. Stevie performed in the school choir. His friends who played musical instruments always wanted to perform for Stevie. They wanted to hear what he thought of their abilities. Stevie was always willing to listen to his friends perform. They would sit in the practice rooms playing music together.

Life on the road made it difficult for Stevie to be at the school much, however. "We set a rule of thumb," Ted Hall remembered. "If we were in the state and available for, let's say, thirty days, I would do the best I could to get Stevie in school for two weeks out of the four weeks. But I'm sure he averaged fifty percent of the time we were in Michigan at the School for the Blind."

In between school and performing on the road, Stevie recorded songs and albums at the Motown studios. Stevie was still recording songs in the Motown formula. Some songs did well, while others did not. Stevie recorded the single "Work Out, Stevie, Work Out" just four months after "Fingertips," but it reached only thirty-three on the charts. In 1964 Stevie recorded two singles along with a couple of albums. "Castles in the Sand" hit number fifty-two. "Hey, Harmonica Man" hit number twenty-nine. By the fall of 1965, some

Partly as a comment on race and antiwar issues, Stevie covered Bob Dylan's "Blowin' in the Wind."

people in the record business were saying that Stevie had gone as far as he could go musically. Stevie was only fifteen.

Back On Top—This Time to Stay

Late in 1965, Stevie decided he wanted to record "Blowin' in the Wind." This was Bob

Dylan's antiwar song, and not the type of Motown sound that the executives thought Stevie should be singing. Stevie wouldn't budge. He wanted to record "Blowin' in the Wind" and sing it his way, using his vocal and instrumental styles. The song reflected Stevie's feelings about the growing conflict in Vietnam. Stevie was becoming mature in his outlook on life, the war, and race relations, and America's changing social makeup was not lost on this hardworking performer.

"Blowin' in the Wind" reached number nine in America, entered the top thirty in Britain, and hit number one on the R & B charts. Stevie found that his musical style was moving away from the typical Motown sound. He enjoyed singing slow ballads, but he also liked to stretch his rock and roll talents. His voice was suited to both musical styles, and his songwriting was becoming unique.

"I never felt that I strictly embodied the Motown sound," Stevie said. "I mean there weren't too many people around there doing white-folk stuff like 'Blowin' in the Wind' or 'Mr. Tambourine Man' like I was."

Over the next three years, Stevie recorded other artists' songs and included them on his albums. Motown resisted his recording such songs as "Water Boy," "Alfie," and "Traveling Man." These songs spoke of the turmoil surrounding the American civil rights battle going on all across the South. Dr. Martin Luther King Jr. was assassinated in Memphis, Tennessee, one month before Stevie turned eighteen. Riots began to tear apart many cities, including his hometown, Detroit. Stevie could not see these events covered on television news programs. He did, however, feel them emotionally. Stevie understood that he had different colored skin than most other Americans. While he did not see this as a problem, he knew many Americans felt otherwise. Stevie's songs showed the music-listening public and his fans that he was trying to pull all Americans together through his music.

Stevie's popularity and star power helped to bridge some of the anger felt between blacks and whites in America. From 1968 to 1970, Stevie had four songs reach the top ten on the charts: "For Once in My Life" (#2); "My Cherie Amour" (#4); "Yester-Me, Yester-You, Yesterday" (#7); and "Signed, Sealed, Delivered, I'm Yours" (#7). That kind of exposure kept Stevie in the public eye and on the music charts.

Growing Up and Away

Stevie graduated from the Michigan School for the Blind when he was nineteen years old. This was June 1969, and he was a pop star. But Stevie didn't want to be a pop star anymore. He wanted to be his own man. He wanted to be an entertainer. Stevie had a vision about his career that did not connect well with the Motown executives. Motown didn't want their musical acts to work too independently. They wanted to maintain the Motown sound that had made the company so successful. They were used to directing their artists' development, each song that was recorded, and all stage performances. Stevie had other ideas. Motown didn't seem to have a clue as to what Stevie really wanted to do with his music.

Stevie celebrates with his first wife, Syreeta Wright, who was also a singer/songwriter.

In a 1969 interview, Stevie commented on the direction his music was headed. "Have you heard the Temptations' 'Cloud Nine'? It's more or less what we call funkadelic. It's a combination of R & B, psychedelic, and funky African-type beat. I'm experimenting. A lot of things I've done recently are funkadelic."

In late 1969, Stevie released the album *Signed, Sealed & Delivered.* It was released under the Motown record label, but Stevie had produced the album himself. Stevie oversaw every detail of its production. This album represented his first real independence from Motown. The album reflected Stevie's independence completely. For one thing, no two songs sounded the same on this album. Stevie had combined his forward vision to create vocals and arrangements that would seal his stardom forever. Each song was charged with an electricity buzzing from Stevie's enthusiastic voice. On several songs, he played all the instruments. The album was both a masterpiece and a calling card: Stevie was ready to take on the music world on his own terms.

Stevie's inner strength came from his vision and talent, and through the help of his mother. He also had outside inspiration. Stevie had met a woman named Syreeta Wright in 1967. Syreeta once worked as a secretary at Motown. Syreeta was also a singer/songwriter. The two fell in love after a long and close friendship. The lyrics to

"Signed, Sealed, Delivered, I'm Yours" were a collaboration between the two. The lyrics also spoke of their mutual love and respect for each other. On September 14, 1970, Stevie and Syreeta married in Detroit. Little Stevie Wonder had stepped out on his own.

Standing on His Own

5

In 1970, Stevie Wonder produced his second album, *Where I'm Coming From.* The songs contained Motown's influence, but Stevie had become his own musician. It was clear that Stevie— now twenty—was ready to depart from Motown for good. He simply had to choose the right time.

Together, Stevie and Syreeta wrote each song on the new album. The musical difference between *Where I'm*

Coming From and earlier albums was like night and day. Stevie played all the instruments on the album. His new playing style on the drums, piano, and harmonica stretched his talents in ways his fans were unused to hearing. Many critics thought the husband and wife songwriting team was trying to be too different from the music that was already out there. Fans disagreed, and the album was successful. The following May, Stevie would complete his transformation.

Breaking (from) the Mold

When Stevie Wonder turned twenty-one on May 13, 1971, his trust fund was opened to him. The last eleven years had included record sales of many millions. It also included expenses, but most of his money had been saved for him. Stevie now had control of more than a million dollars. Luckily, Stevie had learned how to be cautious with his finances. Ted Hall, his mother, and other friends from Motown had taught Stevie well. These lessons helped Stevie to not get too excited about all this money. He had not learned "champagne tastes," and there was no fear that he would go on a spending spree.

As a minor, Stevie had his mother sign his Motown contracts. Now that he was of legal age, those contracts were no good. Stevie could renegotiate with Motown, or ask that the contracts be torn up. Stevie didn't need to think too hard about his decision. He was ready to move on. The president of Motown Records, Ewart Abner II, recalled their meeting: "He came to me and said, 'I'm twenty-one now. I'm not gonna do what you say anymore. Void my contract.' I freaked."

"Freaked" is the right word, too. If Motown had not seen this coming, then they must have felt like a truck had hit the building. Stevie was possibly their top artist and performer and he had just told them to take a hike. Motown executives were hurt, felt betrayed, and knew that money was walking right out the door. Stevie remembered that day: "They were upset at first. But they began to understand—later. I wasn't growing. I just kept repeating 'The Stevie Wonder Sound,' and it didn't express how I felt about what was happening in the world. I decided to go for something else besides a winning formula. I wanted to see what would happen if I changed."

New York Move

Stevie thought about signing with another record company. He talked with many companies, but in the end he decided to work alone for a

Stevie Wonder jamming in the studio

while. He quickly left Detroit and moved into the Howard Johnson Motor Inn in downtown Manhattan. This was close to the Electric Lady Studios on Eighth Street in Greenwich Village. Rock icon Jimi Hendrix had built the studios. Stevie knew the studios were a laid-back place to practice, play, and record. He bought studio time and began to work on a new sound for a new album, *Music of My Mind.*

Did You Know?

Stevie often worked in the recording studio for more than twenty-four hours at a time. Stevie's blindness helped him ignore the night and day that sighted people often live by.

Once again, Stevie and Syreeta cowrote the lyrics. Stevie began to experiment with synthesizers. Synthesizers are computerized instruments that use electronics to produce sound. Stevie used a Moog synthesizer and an Arp synthesizer. They helped him control every piece of each song's sound. They added the rhythm, horn sections, and string sections to his songs. Stevie then played piano, drums, harmonica, organ, and clavichord. He was a one-man band.

Stevie spent a year in New York. He also spent $250,000 for all that studio time. He recorded

During the sessions for *Music of My Mind,* Stevie started recording with synthesizers.

forty songs. Stevie also met some people who would help him complete *Music of My Mind.* The most important person was Johannen Vigoda, a well-known lawyer in the music business. Vigoda and Stevie got to know each other well, and Stevie hired Vigoda to negotiate his next contract.

New Company, New Album, New Stevie!

Stevie needed other people to help him build his own record company. A lot of this help came from his family. Stevie was always close to his brothers and sister. Now he employed some of them in his music business. Taurus Productions was the record company, and Black Bull, Inc. would publish the records. These names referred to Stevie's astrological sign: Taurus the Bull.

Stevie still needed a company to do his advertising and record distribution. Motown came to Stevie and Vigoda with an offer. Stevie signed a contract with Motown that gave him complete creative control of his music. In return, Motown would get half the songwriting royalties. This deal was unique in the recording business. Stevie would make enough money to do anything he wanted musically and personally. In the meantime, Stevie was writing more songs and getting ready to unleash a mountain of innovative music over the next nine years.

Ups and Downs

In 1972, "Superstition" was released. The song hit number one on the charts with its electronic boogie beat and rough-sounding vocals. Stevie was on the radio all over the United States. He still did not have a white following, though. His music was considered purely an African American sound. Stevie wanted to change this image.

In the meantime, Stevie's marriage to Syreeta broke up. After a year and a half, the couple decided it was best to be friends. Stevie told people little about their split. He was always one to put things in the best light: "I just wasn't ready to get married. You know, it depends on whether the minds are in unison. You have to communicate. And I wasn't really communicating." Stevie was always working at the studios. He rarely slept more than four hours each night. Often he would work for two days straight. These habits surely helped to split the two apart. Nevertheless, Stevie

The Rolling Stones jam out on stage with Stevie Wonder during a 1972 Madison Square Garden show in New York City.

produced Syreeta's next two albums. They remained close friends.

Steve's next album *Talking Book*, which included "Superstition" and "You Are the Sunshine of My Life," came out in 1972. Stevie agreed to promote the album by opening for the Rolling Stones on their tour that same year. Stevie loved playing in huge stadiums. The fans, mostly white, middle-class kids, accepted his music. The tour was a success and quickly tripled Stevie's fan base.

Outspoken Activist

Like many celebrities, Stevie Wonder used the public stage to voice his opinions. Black and white race relations in America were not good in the 1970s. Stevie became outspoken when police shootings of black youths occurred in different American cities. He also lashed out when United States president Richard Nixon cut programs that were helping poor African Americans across the country. Stevie tried as best he could to show that social improvement was good for all races in

America. If people understood each other's opinions, wishes, and dreams, there was a chance they could all get along.

"To my way of thinking," Stevie said, "there are many ways of being handicapped, and they certainly aren't all physical. And the real biggest handicap I see around me every day is in people who lack a sense of communication."

Second Life

Innervisions was released in the summer of 1973. Stevie toured to promote the album. On August 6, Stevie slept in the passenger's seat while his cousin, John Harris, drove their car from Greenville, South Carolina, to Durham, North Carolina. Harris tried to pass a logging truck on the highway. Suddenly the truck swerved into the car. A log fell off the truck and onto the car's roof. Stevie was hit by the log and lay in the front seat bleeding from his head.

Stevie was in a coma for three days. The log cracked his skull, and his head swelled. His long-time publicist, Ira Tucker, sang to him one day. "Nobody could get through to him," Tucker recalled. "I got right down in his ear and sang 'Higher Ground.' His hand was resting on my arm, and after a while his fingers started going in tune with the song. I said, yeah! Yeeaah! This dude is gonna make it!"

Stevie woke from his coma and his recovery began. He had lost his sense of taste and smell. This was terrible for Stevie, as he was already blind. But luckily, both senses returned after many weeks. Stevie was worried about his ability to play music. A friend had brought in a clavinet for Stevie to play. Stevie did not touch it for several weeks. Finally, he picked it up and began to play. His relief that the head injuries had not harmed his musical talents made him smile. He'd be able to go on.

Grammy Awards by the Armful!

In March 1974, Stevie appeared at the Grammy Awards. These are the music industry's most

With Better Midler at his side, Stevie proudly displays one of five Grammys he won in 1974.

prized awards. Stevie dreamed only of touching one to find out what it felt like. He never imagined he would be nominated for a Grammy. But in fact, he was nominated for six! That night in March, Stevie was helped onto the stage five times to collect awards. A few weeks after the Grammys, Stevie performed for the first time since his accident. He sold out New York's Madison Square Garden.

Fulfillingness' First Finale was released the following summer. This was Stevie's fourth one-man album. During the months of recording, Stevie met and fell in love with Yolanda Simmons. They married in the fall and moved into a brownstone house in Manhattan. Stevie and Yolanda's daughter, Aisha Zakia (an African name meaning "strength" and "intelligence"), was born in April 1975.

Stevie returned to the Grammy Awards in 1975 to collect five more Grammys! It seemed like Stevie's musical direction had paid off well. His star power was sealing his place in the music recording history books. He was only twenty-five years old.

Charitable Contributions

Stevie has always given his time and money for social causes. He performed at benefit concerts for children stricken with blindness in Ethiopia. He also performed in Washington, D.C., in 1975 at a benefit called Human Kindness Day, organized by a group of humanitarian foundations. Stevie also performed with John Lennon in several benefits for an organization called One To One to help mentally handicapped children.

A New Contract and New Fame

In August 1975, Stevie signed a new seven-year contract with Motown. Stevie was guaranteed $13 million. This was another huge deal that broke records in the music business. The first album recorded under the new contract was *Songs in the Key of Life.* Critics didn't like this double album, but it hit number one on the U.S. charts. In March 1976, Stevie won another five Grammy Awards, one for Best Album of the Year. Stevie Wonder was a household name now, in homes of many different races.

Stevie also began to spend much more time with Yolanda and young Aisha. Stevie felt that he needed to be with Aisha while she was young. He wanted to enjoy his daughter's youth and childhood. That enjoyment doubled when his son, Keita Sawandi (an African name meaning "worshipper" and "founder"), was born on April 16, 1977.

Stevie worked in the studio on projects and new songs for the next three years. In 1979, he released *Stevie Wonder's Journey Through the Secret Life of Plants.* The songs were a collection of symphonic pieces. This album did not sell well at all. Stevie went on tour for the first time in five years. The tour was also a failure. Stevie tried to make his fans understand where he was coming from: "The true meaning of an artist is to be expressive of his art and to be innovative . . .When I listen to my work and I realize that certain things are too out there, too abstract, I try to make it so that everyone will be able to understand it whether they're young or old." Stevie did not plan on being forgotten by the public.

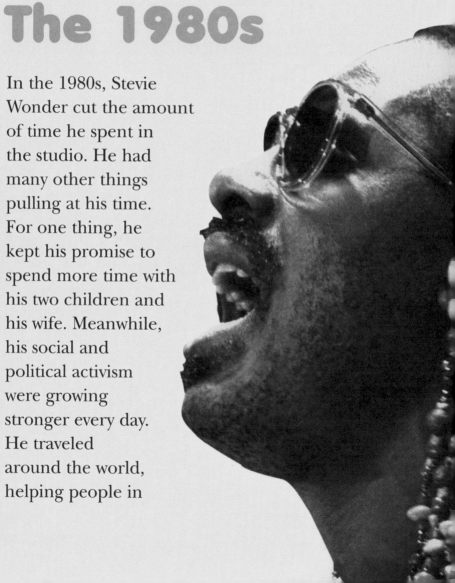

6

The 1980s

In the 1980s, Stevie
Wonder cut the amount
of time he spent in
the studio. He had
many other things
pulling at his time.
For one thing, he
kept his promise to
spend more time with
his two children and
his wife. Meanwhile,
his social and
political activism
were growing
stronger every day.
He traveled
around the world,
helping people in

many ways. By pledging his own money, Stevie showed everyone that they too could make a difference just by giving a little. All through the '80s, Stevie was a tireless worker.

American Musical Tastes

America's music recording industry had Stevie Wonder to thank for a lot of its advancement. In the 1970s, Stevie had introduced many sound change innovations. Synthesizers could speed up beats, stretch chords and notes, and make sounds that no other instruments could ever make. His work with synthesizers paved the way for the disco era and today's hip-hop sound.

Stevie had also helped to break down the color barrier in the radio business. Before his superstar status, African American recording artists were rarely heard on mainstream radio. Stevie's popularity with white America changed all of that. The 1970s burst with African American artists. Stevie's popularity helped such groups as the Jackson Five and Sly and the Family Stone.

By 1983, however, the rhythm and beat of both R & B and pop music had changed. Michael

Stevie embraces South African leader Nelson Mandela, who was jailed for decades for opposing apartheid.

Jackson's *Thriller* exploded onto the charts. *Thriller* set a new record for album sales. It beat the record set by Stevie in the 1970s. Music videos were all the rage, too. The new medium for music was becoming television. Now fans could watch their favorite artists perform their favorite songs every day! Stevie's talents didn't seem suited to video, though. His blindness hindered him from performing for the camera. Michael Jackson had dancers around him. Stevie sat at a piano. He could not get up and move around freely like other artists making videos. Stevie had always thrived on performing for live audiences. Performing in front of a camera without an audience did not work well for his musical talent.

None of this stopped Stevie from recording. He continued to write and record songs. In fact, he has built a huge collection of unreleased music. This library is greater than even Jimi Hendrix's (the king of unreleased recordings). Stevie's image also underwent a transformation with all the change in the early '80s music world. At thirty-three years old, Stevie was now an elder of the recording industry. He became a teacher and guru. He began to produce records for other artists under his own label, Wondirection. The first record produced was for rapper Gary Byrd, whom Stevie saw as a new voice in the African American music scene. Byrd's song "The Crown" included Stevie's music. Stevie began to wonder if his role in music had changed forever.

Motown Reunion and
Saturday Night Live

In 1983, Motown records turned twenty-five. The company produced a television special for the event. Stevie received standing ovations for "I Wish," "You Are the Sunshine of My Life," and "My Cherie Amour." Although Stevie had not released an album in years, the public had not forgotten him.

Stevie had possibly his best time in 1983 when he hosted *Saturday Night Live.* Few people knew that Stevie was a great comedian. He had been keeping his family in stitches almost his whole life. The cast of *Saturday Night Live* (including Eddie Murphy and Joe Piscopo) discovered his talents quickly. Stevie parodied his musical style, his blindness, and racial prejudice. He had a ball doing it, too. Some critics didn't think Stevie should have made fun of his handicap or played a slave plantation owner. Stevie disagreed. He said, "My own feeling was that the whole show is such an obvious joke in the first place, that if you are

Stevie has been a longtime friend and supporter of Jesse Jackson, and even helped him campaign.

going to participate, you have to be that way. And it was fun."

Jesse Jackson and the Martin Luther King Jr. Holiday

Stevie's activism took the national stage during the 1983–1984 presidential election. Stevie supported Jesse Jackson's bid for the presidency. This put African American politics on a national scale for the first time since the civil rights movement in the 1960s. Stevie was, and still is, a hard-working supporter of national African American politics. He understands that many of America's big city populations have an African American majority. Along with Jesse Jackson, Stevie called for political activism in African American communities. By organizing, Stevie argued, African Americans could better their lives. And that would better the lives of all Americans.

Stevie took the national political stage for another reason. He had been working to get Martin Luther King Jr. recognized for his work. Stevie and other activists wanted a national holiday named for King. They were asking for King's birthday, January 20, to be named as the holiday date. A United States Senate vote was held the day after Stevie began a concert series at New York City's Radio City Music Hall. The vote was cast and King would be honored. Today, America celebrates Martin Luther King Jr. day on the third Monday of January each year.

Banned in South Africa

When Stevie accepted the best song Oscar for "I Just Called to Say I Love You" in March 1985, (from the movie *The Woman in Red*) he dedicated his award to the South African activist and antiapartheid leader Nelson Mandela. Mandela was still in prison at this time, and Stevie angered South African radio stations. They stopped playing all of Stevie's music.

Stevie spoke at a press conference the day after the victorious vote: "Somewhere Dr. King is smiling, not because his birthday is a holiday; but because he, too, is convinced that we are moving in the right direction. I know that Dr. King appreciates that this day is a day for all Americans to celebrate love, peace and unity. It is not a cure-all, but it is a healing aid."

Stevie was one of the performers on "We Are the World," a benefit to help starving people in Ethiopia.

Oscar-Winning Song and Hunger Benefit

Stevie had worked on the movie soundtrack to *The Woman in Red* during 1984. The song "I Just Called to Say I Love You" reached number one on the charts, Stevie's first number one hit

since 1977! The song was nominated for an
Academy Award.

Stevie's roots in helping Africa's people
stretched back nearly ten years. When reports of
Ethiopia's starving children reached the world,
money and food began to pour in from around
the world. In America, three generations of
musicians gathered to record "We Are the
World." Dozens of artists—including Ray Charles,
Bruce Springsteen, Michael Jackson, Dionne
Warwick, Madonna, and Bob Dylan—worked
together to make Lionel Richie and Michael
Jackson's song a success. Stevie sat at his piano
and helped coordinate the musical arrangements.
He was there throughout the recording and often
helped get the best singing from these megastars.

Hall of Fame Honors

In 1989, Stevie Wonder was chosen by the Rock
and Roll Hall of Fame Foundation to be
inducted into the Rock and Roll Hall of Fame.
The Rock and Roll Hall of Fame and Museum is

in Cleveland, Ohio. It was started in 1985 as a way of remembering the musicians who helped build rock and roll music and the business of rock and roll. At the Hall of Fame, fans find memorabilia and exhibits honoring hall of famers, and are able to listen to music from the last fifty years.

Stevie Wonder accepted his Hall of Fame honors in New York City. He told the crowd that he felt blessed to have given so much beauty to the world in the form of music. The crowd of fans and musical peers gave Stevie a standing ovation.

Always New Directions

7

As the 1990s began, Stevie continued working with other artists. He appeared on albums, sang at concerts, and worked in his studio. His fans wondered if Stevie was going to continue this sort of career. The soundtrack album for *The Woman in Red* was already five years old. Fans hoped that Stevie was going to thrill them with something new soon.

Stevie's activism was never far behind his music. In fact, they often worked hand in hand. The late 1980s saw Stevie playing at benefit concerts for AIDS awareness and drug abuse, and fund-raising for the blind, mentally handicapped, and homeless. In the 1990s, Stevie traveled the world promoting awareness for each of these social problems. In 1995, Stevie came through for his music fans. He released his long-awaited (and years in the making) *Conversation Peace*.

Peace of Mind

Stevie Wonder's fans might have thought their favorite singer was too busy to write new music. They saw him traveling around the world and respected his humanitarian work. They wanted his music to continue, though. His fans liked his guest-starring roles on other people's albums. Those kept Stevie in the light of the music world. His fans wanted more of Stevie. They wanted the Stevie sound to once again turn their ears toward something new.

In 1995, *Conversation Peace* was released. This album took eight years to complete. Stevie had been writing most of the songs in the late 1980s. The songs describe what he felt about the world around him. *Conversation Peace* was not a summation of Stevie's career, however. He was only forty-five years old at the time of the album's release. There was a lot more music left in Steveland Morris.

Conversation Peace is as complete a statement as any work of art. It tells where Stevie has come from and where he is headed musically. The roots of his R & B sound are on each track. Stevie liked sampling different instrument sounds. This was again Stevie's innovation on *Conversation Peace.* Stevie's voice had never been better than it was on this album. His lyrics were solid, from-the-heart statements of human living, loving, and peace seeking. His music was different than what he'd done earlier, yet showed that he had more creativity within him.

Stevie recalled his musical style on *Conversation Peace* in a 1996 interview: "The only way that you can really stay innovative in music is to be in love with life. You have to live life to be innovative in music. You just have to go through different experiences. I'm not saying you know, go and hang out at some place where you can see somebody get shot in a drive-by. I'm saying you have to, you have to look at yourself over and over again. You have to look back and reflect on how you were, and look at yourself . . . "

In 1997, Stevie followed up *Conversation Peace* with *Natural Wonder*. *Natural Wonder* was recorded live during a Japanese concert tour. Stevie was able to use enough tracks to put out a double CD set. Once again, Stevie was able to show his musical genius by changing song arrangements. He played his older songs with different tempo and harmony. This gave the songs a freshness that Stevie had been looking for.

A Lifetime of Work

By 1997, Stevie Wonder had been making music for nearly thirty-five years. Many people would think of retiring after such an outstanding career. Artists don't retire, though. Their work is all about the life that is happening around

Flanked by his children Keita and Aisha, Stevie accepts a Grammy for lifetime achievement.

them. Artists are always working at a different way to view the world, themselves, and their work. The fans want artists to work, too, but they also want to take the opportunity to reward an artist's achievements.

Stevie's opportunities for fan, industry, and society appreciation began in 1996. He collected a Grammy Award for his lifetime achievement in

President Bill Clinton congratulates Stevie on receiving a lifetime achievement award in 1999.

music. Those achievements spoke well of his musical gifts: Stevie amassed more than twenty number-one hits over his career; he had earned seventeen Grammy Awards, and in 1999 would earn two more!

A few months later, Stevie received an honorary doctorate degree from the University of Alabama at Birmingham. This was the site of

Sighted for the Millennium

On November 15, 1999, Stevie Wonder told a church group of 400 people that he was considering an operation on his eyes. A new medical operation would place a computer chip in his eyes. The chip would help the eyes grow healthy cells. These cells would let Stevie see light and shades. Stevie had this to say: "I've always said that if ever there's a possibility of me seeing, then by whatever means that would take, obviously under the blessings of God, then I would take that challenge."

Some people who have this operation are able to see shapes and some light. A doctor told Stevie, however, that this operation would probably not help him. Without even going through an examination, Stevie decided that he would not undergo the operation.

the future Stevie Wonder Center for Computing in the Arts. Stevie donated a lot of money in order for students to have a place to study music. Traditional music is taught at the center, but music is also explored through interactive multimedia computer training. This is one place where the future of music and the music industry will be on the cutting edge of technology.

In 1999, the Kennedy Center in Washington, D.C., awarded Stevie a lifetime achievement honor. This award is the nation's highest award for artistic achievement. The president of the United States, Bill Clinton, appeared at this ceremony and awarded this prestigious honor to Stevie.

Keys to the City

Stevie returned to Detroit in July 2001 to perform at a free concert celebrating Detroit's 300th anniversary as a city. His performance was a testament to all Detroit natives and music lovers. Stevie Wonder was a hometown sensation.

A New Century, the Same Love

The new millennium saw Stevie working harder than ever for charities. Stevie has supported charities fighting child hunger, disease, homelessness, and poverty for more than twenty years. On November 8, 2000, *Music of Love* with a song by Stevie was released. This album was a special tribute by various recording stars to benefit children around the world. Money made on the album went to UNICEF, an organization that helps children all around the world.

Just one month later, Stevie hosted the Toys Benefit Concert. The concert took place at the Great Western Forum in Los Angeles. Fans coming to the concert were asked to bring a new toy as a donation.

A Look into the Future

Stevie Wonder's future will be much like his recent past: He plans to continue producing, writing, and recording music. He even plans to write an autobiography. No tours are planned,

In addition to his own concerts, Stevie has made appearances at dozens of benefits and special events.

but Stevie always seems to show up at a benefit concert or special event. He is known for showing up on stage with some of today's most famous musicians. This is Stevie's life, and he is happy with the success and fun that it has given him. Stevie is a much more private person than he once was. Whether this is because music has moved in so many directions since his glory years in the 1970s is a subject for debate. Stevie easily puts his life and music in focus: "You know that you're going to have moments when there will be personal things that deal with just your personal life that are significant only to yourself. You still have to face the audience and do the performance. But as much as possible, if you realize that being yourself is being the artist that you are, then who you are pretty much comes from what you are as a person."

SELECTED DISCOGRAPHY

1967 *I Was Made to Love Her*
1968 *For Once In My Life*
1969 *My Cherie Amour*
1970 *Signed, Sealed & Delivered*
1972 *Music of My Mind*
1972 *Talking Book*
1973 *Innervisions*
1974 *Fulfillingness' First Finale*
1976 *Songs in the Key of Life*
1979 *Stevie Wonder's Journey Through the Secret Life of Plants*
1980 *Hotter Than July*
1982 *Stevie Wonder's Original Musiquarium I*
1984 *The Woman in Red*
1985 *In Square Circle*
1987 *Characters*
1991 *Jungle Fever*
1995 *Conversation Peace*
1995 *Natural Wonder*
1999 *At the Close of a Century*

GLOSSARY

accommodate To allow someone a way to do something that would otherwise be difficult to complete.

activist Someone who speaks out and works for a good cause.

arrangement In music, to play or sing a song a certain way (for instance fast or slow, loud or soft).

charts Published lists of the top-selling singles or albums.

choir A large group of people who sing songs together.

conductor The person who directs a song.

echo When sound bounces off a distant object.

facial expressions The different faces humans and animals make to express their feelings.

formula A set way of doing something.

funkadelic A type of music, originated in the 1970s, that combined different styles of music.

guru Someone who knows something so well that he or she is seen as the best teacher.

harmony The smooth flow of musical notes.

icon An object or person that receives devotion from fans or followers.

improvise To invent music or a song as you are playing or singing.

incubator A plastic container that holds newborn babies and helps them breathe.

influence To steer someone toward a way of doing something.

jamming Playing music with others, without following a set song.

lyrics The words to a song.

minor Someone who is under the legal adult age.

renegotiate To make a new deal (contract) after the terms of the old one have expired.

retrolental fibroplasia A harmful disease caused by too much oxygen given to

babies at birth when they are put in an
incubator.

rhythm and blues (R & B) A kind of music
begun in the 1950s by African American artists.

style One way of doing something, such as a
certain way of singing or playing a song.

talent The ability to do something well.

TO FIND OUT MORE

Motown Records
1755 Broadway, 7th Floor
New York, NY 10019
Web site: http://www.motown.com

Rock and Roll Hall of Fame Foundation
1290 Avenue of the Americas
New York, NY 10104

Rock and Roll Hall of Fame and Museum
One Key Plaza
Cleveland, OH 44114
(888) 764-ROCK (7625)
Web site: http://www.rockhall.com

Web Sites

Stevie Wonder: The Web Site
http://www.stevie-wonder.com

The Unofficial Stevie Wonder Web Site
http://www.insoul.com/stevie

FOR FURTHER READING

Horn, Martin E. *Stevie Wonder: Career of a Rock Legend.* New York: Arrowood Press, 1996.

King, Coretta. *Stevie Wonder: Musician.* Broomall, PA: Chelsea House Publishers, 1995.

DeLisa, Jeannette, ed. *Stevie Wonder: Conversation Peace.* New York: Warner Brothers Publications, 1995.

Swenson, John. *Stevie Wonder.* New York: Harper & Row, 1986.

Works Cited

Driscoll, O'Connell. "Growing Up Stevie Wonder." *Rolling Stone,* June 19, 1975, p. 44.

Haskins, James. *The Story of Stevie Wonder.* New York: Lothrop, Lee & Shepard Books, 1976.

Levitin, Daniel J. "Conversation Peace." *Grammy Magazine,* Vol. 14, No. 3, Summer 1996, pp. 14–25.

Orth, Maureen. "Stevie, The Wonder Man." *Newsweek,* October 28, 1974, pp. 59–62.

Slater, Jack. "A Sense of Wonder." *The New York Times Magazine*, February 23, 1975, pp. 18–19.

Snider, Burr. "Hey, Stevie Wonder, How's Your Bad Self?" *Esquire*, April 1974, pp. 100–102.

Swenson, John. *Stevie Wonder*. New York: Harper & Row, 1986.

INDEX

CREDITS

About The Author

Mark Beyer has written more than forty young adult and children's books. He also writes novels and poetry. Mark lives with his wife in New York City.

Photo Credits

Design

Thomas Forget

Layout

Tahara Hasan